SUMMARY OF PROCEEDINGS

Background

As mandated by the Small Business Investment Incentive Act of 1980, the U.S. Securities and Exchange Commission conducts an annual forum that focuses on small business capital formation.[1] Called the "SEC Government-Business Forum on Small Business Capital Formation," this gathering has assembled every year since 1982. A major purpose of the Forum is to provide a platform to highlight perceived unnecessary impediments to small business capital formation and address whether they can be eliminated or reduced. Each Forum seeks to develop recommendations for government and private action to improve the environment for small business capital formation, consistent with other public policy goals, including investor protection.

The 2013 Forum, the 32nd, was convened at the SEC's headquarters at 100 F Street, N.E., Washington, D.C., on Thursday, November 21, 2013. The program included both panel discussions and breakout groups.

Planning and Organization

Consistent with the SEC's statutory mandate in the Small Business Investment Incentive Act of 1980, the SEC's Office of Small Business Policy (part of its Division of Corporation Finance) invited other federal government agencies, the North American Securities Administrators Association ("NASAA," the organization representing state securities regulators), and leading small business and professional organizations concerned with small business capital formation to participate in planning the 2013 Forum. The individuals who participated in planning the Forum, and their professional affiliations, are listed on pages 4 through 6.

The planning group recommended that this year's Forum again be held in Washington, D.C. The members of the planning group also assisted in preparing the agenda and in recruiting speakers.

Participants

The SEC's Office of Small Business Policy worked with members of the planning group to identify potential panel participants for the 2013 Forum. Invitations to attend the Forum were sent to participants in previous Forums and to members of various business and professional organizations concerned with small business capital formation. In addition, the SEC's Office of Minority and Women Inclusion assisted in reaching out and extending invitations to representatives from several diverse business communities, including minority-owned businesses, women-owned businesses and veteran-owned

---

[1] The SEC is required to conduct the Forum annually and to prepare this report under 15 U.S.C. 80c-1 (codifying section 503 of Pub. L. No. 96-477, 94 Stat. 2275 (1980)).

businesses. The SEC issued two press releases to inform the public about the time, date and location of the Forum.

The morning panel discussions were accessible through a live webcast on the SEC's website. A written transcript of the panel discussions and other morning proceedings has been posted on the SEC website. The afternoon breakout group sessions were not webcast, but were accessible by conference telephone call to pre-registered participants.

Approximately 175 attendees were physically present for the Forum proceedings in Washington, plus approximately 14 panelists and moderators, including an SEC Commissioner and SEC senior staff.

Proceedings

The agenda for the 2013 Forum is reprinted starting on page 8. The Forum's morning proceedings began with opening remarks by Keith F. Higgins, Director of the SEC Division of Corporation Finance. Two panel discussions were then conducted on evolving practices in the new world of Regulation D offerings, moderated by Gregory C. Yadley and Keith F. Higgins, and on what might be next for small businesses and markets once the JOBS Act is fully implemented, moderated by David M. Lynn and Keith F. Higgins.

The afternoon proceedings included breakout group meetings open to all pre-registered participants, who took part both in person and by telephone conference call. Three breakout groups met, one on securities-based crowdfunding offerings, which was moderated by Douglas S. Ellenoff, a second on exempt securities offerings, which was moderated by Gregory C. Yadley, and a third on the securities regulation of smaller public companies, which was moderated by Spencer G. Feldman.

The discussions of the three breakout groups resulted in draft recommendations. The moderators of the three breakout groups presented their respective groups' recommendations at a final assembly of all the Forum participants as the last matter of business on November 21, 2013.

After the Forum, the moderators of the three breakout groups continued to work with their group participants to refine each group's recommendations. A final list of 43 recommendations resulting from these discussions was circulated by e-mail to all participants in the three breakout groups, asking them to specify whether, in their view, the SEC should give high, medium, low or no priority to each recommendation. This poll resulted in the prioritized list of 43 recommendations presented starting on page 10.

Records of Proceedings and Previous Forum Materials

A video recording of the Forum's morning proceedings, including the two panel discussions, is available on the SEC's website at http://www.sec.gov/news/otherwebcasts/2013/gbforum112113.shtml. A transcript of the morning proceedings is available on the SEC's website at http://www.sec.gov/info/smallbus/sbforumtrans-112113.pdf.

The Forum program, including the biographies of the Forum panelists and moderators, is available on the SEC's website at http://www.sec.gov/info/smallbus/forum-program-112113.pdf.

The final reports and other materials relating to previous Forums, dating back to 1993, may be found on the SEC's website at http://www.sec.gov/info/smallbus/sbforum.shtml.

PLANNING GROUP

Moderator

Gerald J. Laporte
Former Chief, Office of Small Business Policy
Division of Corporation Finance
U.S. Securities and Exchange Commission
Washington, D.C.

Government/Regulatory
  Representatives

Gabriela Aguero
Assistant Director
Corporate Financing Department
Financial Industry Regulatory Authority
Rockville, Maryland

Ammar Askari
Community Development Expert
  Community Affairs
Office of the Comptroller of the
  Currency
Washington, D.C.

Anthony G. Barone
Special Counsel
Office of Small Business Policy
Division of Corporation Finance
U.S. Securities and Exchange
  Commission
Washington, D.C.

William Beatty
Director of Securities
Securities Division
Department of Financial Institutions
Olympia, Washington
Corporate Finance Committee Chair,
  North American Securities
  Administrators Association, Inc.

Mauri L. Osheroff
Former Associate Director
(Regulatory Policy)
Division of Corporation Finance
U.S. Securities and Exchange
  Commission
Washington, D.C.

Robin A. Prager
Senior Adviser
Division of Research and Statistics
Board of Governors of the Federal
  Reserve System
Washington, D.C.

Mary J. Sjoquist
Director
Office of Outreach and Small Business
  Liaison
Public Company Accounting Oversight
  Board
Washington, D.C.

Dillon J. Taylor
Assistant Chief Counsel for Advocacy
Office of Advocacy
U.S. Small Business Administration
Washington, D.C.

Representatives of Business and
Professional Organizations

Brian T. Borders
Borders Law Group
Washington, D.C.
Representing National Venture Capital
  Association

4

Michael J. Choate
Shefsky & Froelich, Ltd.
Chicago, Illinois
*Representing Legal Committee of the
Investment Program Association*

Charles Crain
Manager, Policy & Research
Biotechnology Industry Organization
Washington, D.C.

Deborah S. Froling
Arent Fox
Washington, D.C.
*Member of the Board of Directors of the
Real Estate Investment Securities
Association*

Stacey Geer
Senior Vice President and
 Associate General Counsel
Primerica, Inc.
Duluth, Georgia
*Chair of the Small and Mid Cap
 Companies Committee of the
Society of Corporate Secretaries and
 Governance Professionals*

Martin A. Hewitt
Attorney at Law
East Brunswick, New Jersey
*Representing Am. Bar Ass'n Business
 Law Section Task Force on Private
 Placement Broker Dealers*

Shane B. Hansen
Warner Norcross & Judd, LLP
Grand Rapids, Michigan
*Representing State Regulation of
 Securities Committee of American Bar
 Association*

Kevin M. Hogan
President and CEO
Investment Program Association
New York, New York

Marianne Hudson
Executive Director
Angel Capital Association
Overland Park, Kansas

Andrew Huff
Office Manager and
 Legislative Assistant
National Association of Small Business
 Investment Companies
Washington, D.C.

John J. Huntz
Executive Director
Head of Venture Capital
Arcapita, Inc.
Atlanta, Georgia
*Chairman and Founder of Atlanta
 Venture Forum*

James Kendrick
Vice President, Accounting & Capital
 Policy
Independent Community Bankers of
 America
Washington, D.C.

Karen Kerrigan
President & CEO
Small Business & Entrepreneurship
 Council (SBE Council), and
Founder, WE Inc. (Women
 Entrepreneurs)
Oakton, Virginia

David Marlett
Managing Partner
Crowdfund International
Dallas, Texas
*Founder and Executive Director of the
 National Crowdfunding Association*

Vincent Molinari
Co-Founder, CEO & Chairman
Gate Global Impact
New York, New York
*Co-Chair of Crowdfund
Intermediary Regulatory Advocates*

Shelly Mui-Lipnik
Senior Director
Tax and Financial Services
Biotechnology Industry Organization
Washington, D.C.

A. John Murphy
Wickersham & Murphy
Palo Alto, California
*Representing Federal Regulation of
Securities Committee of American Bar
Association*

Cristeena Naser
Vice President and Senior Counsel
Center for Securities, Trust &
  Investments
American Bankers Association
Washington, D.C.

Brett T. Palmer
President
Small Business Investor Alliance
Washington, D.C.

E.J. Reedy
Manager
Research and Policy
Kauffman Foundation

Timothy A. Reese
Managing Partner
National Minority Angel Network
Ambler, Pennsylvania

Andrew J. Sherman
Jones Day
Washington, D.C. and
Adjunct Professor of Business and
  Capital Formation Strategy
Smith School of Business
University of Maryland
College Park, Maryland
*General Counsel to Entrepreneurs'
Organization and Small and Emerging
Contractors Advisory Forum*

Kevin Wells
Senior Manager
Center for Capital Markets
  Competitiveness
U.S. Chamber of Commerce
Washington, D.C.

Gregory C. Yadley
Shumaker, Loop & Kendrick, LLP
Tampa, Florida
*Representing Committee on Middle
Market and Small Business of
American Bar Association*

SEC STAFF

Elizabeth M. Murphy
Associate Director (Legal)
Division of Corporation Finance

Office of Small Business Policy
Division of Corporation Finance

Sebastian Gomez Abero, Chief

Karen C. Wiedemann, Former Attorney Fellow

Anthony G. Barone, Special Counsel

Zachary O. Fallon, Special Counsel

Johanna Vega Losert, Special Counsel

Shehzad K. Niazi, Attorney-Advisor

William Mastrianna, Former Student Intern

AGENDA

2013 SEC Government-Business Forum on Small Business Capital Formation
Washington, D.C.
November 21, 2013

9:00 a.m.   **Call to Order**
Mauri L. Osheroff, Associate Director, SEC Division of Corporation Finance

Opening Remarks
Keith F. Higgins, Director, SEC Division of Corporation Finance

9:20 a.m.   **Panel Discussion: Evolving Practices in the New World of Regulation D Offerings**

Moderators:

Keith F. Higgins, Director, SEC Division of Corporation Finance
Gregory C. Yadley, Partner, Shumaker, Loop & Kendrick, LLP, Tampa, Florida

Panelists:

Christopher Mirabile, Board Member, Angel Capital Association;
Co-Managing Director, LaunchPad Venture Group, LLC, Boston, Massachusetts
John H. Chory, Partner, Latham & Watkins, LLP, Boston, Massachusetts
Troy Foster, Partner, Wilson, Sonsini, Goodrich & Rosati, LLP, Palo Alto, California
Rick A. Fleming, Deputy General Counsel, North American Securities Administrators Association, Inc., Washington, D.C.

10:45 a.m.   **Break**

11:05 a.m.   **Panel Discussion: Crystal Ball: Now that You Raised the Money, What's Next for the Company and the Markets?**

Moderators:

Keith F. Higgins, Director, SEC Division of Corporation Finance
David M. Lynn, Partner, Morrison & Foerster, LLP, Washington, D.C.

SEC Commissioner Kara M. Stein

Panelists:

Kim Wales, Founder and CEO, Wales Capital, New York, New York
Douglas S. Ellenoff, Partner, Ellenoff, Grossman & Schole, LLP, New York, New York
John D. Hogoboom, Partner, Lowenstein Sandler PC, Roseland, New Jersey
Annemarie Tierney, Executive Vice President, Legal Affairs and General Counsel, SecondMarket, New York, New York

12:30 pm.   **Lunch Break**

2:00 p.m.   **Breakout Group Meetings**

    ▶ **Securities-Based Crowdfunding Offerings Breakout Group**

    Moderator:

        Douglas S. Ellenoff, Partner, Ellenoff, Grossman & Schole, LLP, New York, New York

    ▶ **Exempt Securities Offerings Breakout Group**

    Moderator:

        Gregory C. Yadley, Partner, Shumaker, Loop & Kendrick, LLP, Tampa, Florida

    ▶ **Securities Regulation of Smaller Public Companies Breakout Group**

    Moderator:

        Spencer G. Feldman, Partner, Greenberg Traurig, New York, NewYork

3:15 p.m.   **Break**

3:30 p.m.   **Breakout Group Meetings (continued)**

4:45 p.m.   **Plenary Session to Develop Next Steps**

Moderators:

Mauri L. Osheroff, Associate Director, SEC Division of Corporation Finance
Gregory C. Yadley, Partner, Shumaker, Loop & Kendrick, LLP, Tampa, Florida

5:30 p.m.   **Networking Reception**

CONSOLIDATED FORUM RECOMMENDATIONS[2]

Set forth below are the 43 recommendations of the 2013 SEC Government-Business Forum on Small Business Capital Formation, consolidated from the three breakout groups of the Forum held on the afternoon of November 21, 2013. The three breakout groups covered the following topics: Securities-Based Crowdfunding Offerings, Exempt Securities Offerings, and Securities Regulation of Smaller Public Companies. After that date, the moderators of the breakout groups worked with their breakout group participants to refine each group's recommendations.

The recommendations are presented below in the order of priority established as the result of a poll of all participants in the breakout groups.[3] The priority ranking is intended to provide guidance to the SEC as to the importance and urgency the poll respondents assigned to each recommendation.

For additional clarity with respect to the interest in each broad area of discussion, the recommendations are also presented starting on page 19 by the breakout groups from which they originated.[4]

---

[2] The SEC conducts the SEC Government-Business Forum on Small Business Capital Formation, but does not endorse or modify any of the recommendations of the Forum. The recommendations are solely the responsibility of the Forum participants, who were responsible for developing them. The recommendations do not necessarily reflect the views of the SEC, its Commissioners or any of the SEC's staff members.

[3] In the poll, the participants were asked to respond whether the SEC should give "high," "medium," "low" or "no" priority to each of the 43 recommendations. Of the 126 participants, 34 responded, a 27% response rate. Each "high priority" response was assigned five points, each "medium priority" was assigned three points, each "low priority" response was assigned one point and each "no priority" or blank response was assigned zero points. The total number of points assigned to each recommendation is shown in brackets after the text of the recommendation, as is the average assignment of points for the recommendation. The average assignment of points was determined for each recommendation by dividing the total number of points for a recommendation by the number of responses received (34).

[4] Of the 34 respondents to the poll, 17 were participants in the Securities-Based Crowdfunding Offerings Breakout Group, 14 were participants in the Exempt Securities Offerings Breakout Group and 7 were participants in the Securities Regulation of Smaller Public Companies Breakout Group. Four respondents participated in more than one breakout group.

1   We recommend that the Commission withdraw its proposed amendments to Regulation D, Form D and Rule 156. If the Commission determines not to do so, then we urge that revised proposals be published for further comment to include the following:

☐   Removal of the harsh penalties for non-compliance;
☐   No requirement for an advance Form D, instead require filing no earlier than the date of first sale and a closing or annual filing (if sales were made);
☐   Allow parts of Form D, such as the financing amount, to be confidential;
☐   Require legends and disclosures only when sale terms are communicated;
☐   Rather than requiring the filing of advertising materials, form working groups from advisory bodies to monitor and report to the Commission; and
☐   Clarify the meaning of "general solicitation," and confirm that longstanding economic development events, such as "demo days," do not constitute general solicitation. [112 points; avg. ranking 3.29]

2   Because Rule 506(c) exempt offerings exclude non-accredited friends and family investors, who have traditionally been important participants in small business capital formation, we recommend that the Commission:

☐   Maintain the ability of Rule 506(c) issuers to concurrently offer Section 4(a)(6) crowdfunding securities, as set forth in the proposed rules issued pursuant to the JOBS Act; and
☐   Clarify that an issuer changing from a Rule 506(b) offering to a Rule 506(c) offering may sell to friends and family and other non-accredited investors in a parallel Section 4(a)(6) crowdfunding offering. [105 points; avg. ranking 3.09]

3   We recommend that the Commission not increase the dollar amount thresholds in the accredited investor definition following its review of the definition, as mandated by the Dodd-Frank Act. The Commission has effectively already increased the financial threshold in the definition by removing the value of the primary residence, which resulted in a significant drop in the investor pool from 9% to 7% of U.S. households, thus limiting both capital formation and job creation. At the same time, we recommend that the Commission consider additional separate categories of qualification for accredited investors based on various types of sophistication, for example, by virtue of education, experience or training. [101 points; avg. ranking 2.97]

4	Eliminate the requirement for audited financial statements in crowdfunding offerings, and instead require that financial statements for offerings of $500,000 or more be reviewed by a certified public accountant. [100 points; avg. ranking 2.94]
5	The Commission should provide clarification and a framework on what is considered investment advice for a crowdfunding portal. Portals should be able to provide a labeling mechanism, such as an issue is "hot" or "trending," along with an advanced search feature. [98 points; avg. ranking 2.88]
6A	Based on recent changes resulting from the JOBS Act, private companies will have much more flexibility to remain private longer. As a result, the need for a specific federal exemption for private secondary transactions for shareholders that cannot satisfy Rule 144 has become critical. We recommend that the Commission propose a new federal exemption governing the private resale of restricted securities under Section 4(a)(1) of the Securities Act, commonly referred to as "Section 4(1-1/2)" (or after the JOBS Act amendments to the Securities Act, Section 4(a)(1-1/2)). [95 points; avg. ranking 2.79]
6B	The Commission should promptly adopt rules implementing Title IV of the JOBS Act that preempt state law review and regulation (but not enforcement) for the issuance of securities thereunder. The Commission should consider, among other means of accomplishing this:

       ☐   Making a security offered in reliance upon the Regulation A+ exemption a "covered security" under Section 18(b) of the Securities Act;

       ☐   Adopting a "qualified purchaser" definition under Section 18(b)(3) of the Securities Act to include purchasers of securities sold in reliance upon the Regulation A+ exemption;

       ☐   Preempting only state regulation that fails to comply with uniform state regulation guidelines adopted by NASAA in consultation with the Commission; or

       ☐   Seeking any legislation necessary to so preempt state regulation.

New regulations promulgated under Title IV of the JOBS Act should provide for scaled disclosure based on, among other factors, size of offering, including unaudited financial statements for smaller offerings, and encourage user-friendly techniques, such as Q&A. [95 points; avg. ranking 2.79]

6C	The Commission should provide guidelines to crowdfunding intermediaries as to what constitutes curating deals. [95 points; avg. ranking 2.79]
9	Eliminate the imposition of liability against a crowdfunding platform for the misstatements and omissions of the companies that post on the platform's website,

which is proposed in the SEC proposing release for Title III of the JOBS Act at Section II.E.5 of Release No. 33-9470 (Oct. 23, 2013).
[94 points; avg. ranking 2.76]

10   Repeal the requirement for smaller reporting companies and emerging growth companies to submit financial information in XBRL format for periodic reports and other public filings. [92 points; avg. ranking 2.71]

11   Allow crowdfunding portals to create a membership tiered system that will disclose only specific company details (e.g., financial statements) to registered members on the platform. [85 points; avg. ranking 2.50]

12   In the voting and prioritization phase of this Forum, the recommendations of each breakout group should be presented separately from those of the other two breakout groups. [83 points; avg. ranking 2.44]

13A   Revise the definition of "smaller reporting company" under the Securities Act and Exchange Act to include companies with:

☐   A public float of up to $250 million; or
☐   Annual revenues of up to $100 million, so long as their public float is not more than $700 million.

These companies are still generally considered "micro-caps."
[81 points; avg. ranking 2.38]

13B   Clarify whether the intent of proposed Rule 203 of Regulation Crowdfunding is to require all material information to be filed on proposed Form C, or whether "free writing" is permitted to be posted on platforms. [81 points; avg. ranking 2.38]

15A   Allow crowdfunding intermediaries to syndicate deals between platforms by having one lead intermediary host and provide a communication channel to the other funding portals and allow funding portals to share commissions and fees. Transactions must be conducted on the intermediary platform on which they originated. [74 points; avg. ranking 2.18]

15B   Broker-dealers and registered crowdfunding portals should be allowed to share transaction-based compensation in conjunction with Section 4(a)(6) offerings. [74 points; avg. ranking 2.18]

17   Forum participants report that many broker-dealers will not accept, deposit, clear, sell and/or trade low-priced stocks. They note that the Financial Industry Regulatory Authority ("FINRA") and the Depository Trust Company ("DTC") are requiring broker-dealers to take inordinate responsibility and liability for possible

counterfeit certificates, tracking the origin of prior share transfers and monitoring the placement of restricted legends. This issue seriously impacts the participation of investors in financing micro-cap issuers. Through all of its appropriate divisions, the SEC should promptly commence discussions with FINRA and DTC to determine the reasons for, and extent of, these perceived practices, and how such practices can be modified so as not to hamper small business capital formation. [72 points; avg. ranking 2.12]

18   The Commission should join with NASAA and FINRA in the effort to implement the basic principles of the American Bar Association Task Force on Private Placement Brokers. Further, to achieve this goal, the Commission should join NASAA and FINRA in developing a timeframe for quarterly or other regular meetings—with specified benchmarks—until a mutually agreeable regime of finder registration and regulation is achieved. [71 points; avg. ranking 2.09]

19A   Amend the eligibility requirements in the General Instructions of Form S-3 to permit smaller reporting companies, companies whose common equity securities are not listed on a national securities exchange and companies whose shares are defined as "penny stock" to utilize a registration statement on Form S-3 for primary and secondary offerings, but not for automatically effective shelf offerings, if the companies are current in their Exchange Act reports and have timely filed those reports within the past 12 months. The justifications against expanding Form S-3 usage to smaller public companies have been substantially eliminated with advanced information technology, including EDGAR. This recommendation follows closely the SEC's own proposed rule in 2007 to revise the eligibility requirements for primary securities offerings on Form S-3. See *Revisions to the Eligibility Requirements for Primary Securities Offerings on Forms S-3 and F-3*, Release No. 33-8812 (June 20, 2007). [70 points; avg. ranking 2.06]

19B   Standardize baseline educational material across crowdfunding portals in order to establish an industry standard similar to the Real Estate Settlement Procedure Act ("RESPA") administered by the Consumer Financial Protection Bureau ("CFPB") for the mortgage industry. [70 points; avg. ranking 2.06]

21A   Support the ongoing efforts of Nasdaq OMX Group Inc. and NYSE Euronext to widen "tick sizes" to increments of $0.05 for smaller reporting company stock trading. [69 points; avg. ranking 2.03]

21B   Permit "forward incorporation by reference" in registration statements on Form S-1 by all companies. Current practices to supplement an effective registration statement add little or nothing to the availability or quality of subsequent public information provided by issuers. [69 points; avg. ranking 2.03]

21C   In 1988, pursuant to its exemptive authority, the Commission first issued Rule 701 to allow private companies to sell securities to employees for compensatory purposes. In 1999, the Commission added certain disclosure requirements for sales exceeding $5 million in a 12-month period. Given the Section 12(g) exemptions for employees provided in the JOBS Act, an update of these thresholds is appropriate. We recommend that the Commission raise the dollar threshold for triggering the required disclosures pursuant to a Rule 701 offering from $5 million to no less than $10 million. [69 points; avg. ranking 2.03]

24   Crowdfunding platforms of foreign entities should be allowed to conduct business as a U.S. crowdfunding portal only if the foreign entity forms a partnership with a U.S. crowdfunding portal. [68 points; avg. ranking 2.00]

25   Allow crowdfunding intermediaries the ability to monitor misstatements on crowdfunding platforms, monitor Q&A commentary and de-rank accordingly as a filtering mechanism. Allow crowdfunding intermediaries the ability to curate based on less objective factors, such as management team experience, over-inflated financials, or size of funding requested, if the funding request is too little to realistically achieve business goals. [67 points; avg. ranking 1.97]

26   Consider recommending for enactment by Congress an amendment to the definition of an "emerging growth company" ("EGC") in Section 2(a)(19) of the Securities Act to provide the same benefits that are applicable to EGCs pursuant to the JOBS Act to companies that would have qualified as an EGC, but for the fact that their initial public offerings were declared effective on or prior to December 8, 2011. Congress may accomplish this by amending the definition of an EGC in paragraph (B) of Section 2(a)(19) to add language that states companies whose IPOs were declared effective on or prior to December 8, 2011 may be treated as EGCs starting as of the date of this amendment so as to give effectively to these companies a full 5 years of potential EGC eligibility. [66 points; avg. ranking 1.94]

27A   Amend the cover pages of Form 10-K and Form 10-Q to permit registrants to provide the various alternative URL addresses and locations where corporate information may be disseminated by the registrant (e.g., Facebook, Twitter, Tumblr, Instagram and LinkedIn) and, provide that any such postings shall constitute public dissemination for purposes of Regulation FD.
[65 points; avg. ranking 1.91]

27B   Another medium other than the Internet should be made acceptable to perform crowdfunding transactions, particularly for local, community-based capital raising efforts. [65 points; avg. ranking 1.91]

29   Extend the disclosure exemptions and scaled or phased-in disclosure obligations that are provided to EGCs under the JOBS Act to all smaller reporting companies, unless there is a significant policy reason for not doing so, including the following

requirements:

☐   The requirement in Exchange Act Section 14A(a) to conduct shareholder advisory votes on executive compensation and on the frequency of such votes;

☐   The requirement in Exchange Act Section 14A(b) to provide disclosure about and conduct shareholder advisory votes on golden parachute compensation;

☐   The requirement in Section 953(b) of the Dodd-Frank Act, as promulgated by the Commission to be in Item 402 of Regulation S-K, to provide disclosure of the ratio of the median annual total compensation of all employees of the registrant to the annual total compensation of the chief executive officer;

☐   The requirement in Exchange Act Section 14(i) to provide disclosure of the relationship between executive compensation and issuer financial performance;

☐   In the case of a new or revised financial accounting standard that has different compliance dates for public and private companies, the deferral of compliance with any such financial accounting standard until the date that a private company is required to comply; and

☐   Any rules of the Public Company Accounting Oversight Board ("PCAOB") requiring mandatory audit firm rotation or a supplement to the auditor's report in which the auditor would be required to provide additional information about the audit and the financial statements of the registrant. [64 points; avg. ranking 1.88]

30   Prohibit the PCAOB from requiring any report or procedure similar to a supplement to the auditor's report in which the auditor would be required to provide additional information about the audit and the financial statements of the issuer, such as a report on "critical audit matters" for the auditors of smaller reporting companies and EGCs. [62 points; avg. ranking 1.82]

31   Given the dwindling number of market-makers willing to submit FINRA Form 211 for trading the shares of smaller publicly reporting companies on the over-the-counter market, the SEC's Division of Trading and Markets should encourage FINRA to allow payment by an issuer of a fixed fee to a market-maker to compensate the market-maker for its time and effort involved in required due diligence, form preparation and related expenses. [59 points; avg. ranking 1.74]

32   As has been generally recommended since 2008, Rule 144(i) should be amended to provide a shell company relief two years after filing a Form 8-K to report that it is no longer a shell company. [56 points; avg. ranking 1.65]

Priority Rank	Recommendation

33A   Through all applicable divisions of the SEC, take steps with the national securities exchanges to lower to $15 million the current $40 million minimum required size of a public offering following a reverse merger of an issuer to eliminate the so-called "seasoning" requirement that delays listing the securities of that issuer for more than one year, notwithstanding otherwise meeting all other quantitative and qualitative listing requirements. [55 points; avg. ranking 1.62]

33B   Eliminate the applicability to smaller reporting companies of rules mandating disclosure with respect to conflict minerals, as well as reports by natural resource extraction issuers, concerning payments made to a foreign government or the U.S. federal government in order to further the commercial development of oil, natural gas or minerals, as such rules would be cost prohibitive for smaller natural resource companies. [55 points; avg. ranking 1.62]

33C   Add a general instruction to Regulation S-K that permits smaller reporting companies to omit disclosure required pursuant to a line item in Regulation S-K in the event that such disclosure is not material from the perspective of a reasonable investor. This general instruction should contain language similar to that in Rule 502(b)(2) of Regulation D, which limits the disclosure required to be provided to the purchaser by an issuer "to the extent material to an understanding of the issuer, its business, and the securities being offered." This would add an element of principles-based disclosure to Regulation S-K. [55 points; avg. ranking 1.62]

36   Provide a dashboard (tool) that will show updates on intrastate crowdfunding exemptions and federal laws for crowdfunding. [54 points; avg. ranking 1.59]

37   Provide a final rule as to when public companies are required to adopt the new 2013 Framework of the Committee of Sponsoring Organizations of the Treadway Commission ("COSO"), and provide a one-year delay for required implementation of the rule by smaller reporting companies. [53 points; avg. ranking 1.56]

38A   Standardize deal structures across crowdfunding platforms.
[51 points; avg. ranking 1.50]

38B   Develop educational programs aimed at minority owned firms and investors, and track the effectiveness of those efforts. [51 points; avg. ranking 1.50]

40   Anyone that invests in a qualifying business, such as a minority, women or veteran owned business, should become eligible for income tax relief based on their investment. [49 points; avg. ranking 1.44]

41   The SEC should repeal the requirement to file an information statement pursuant to Section 14(f) of the Exchange Act and Rule 14f-1 thereunder, concerning notice of change in the majority of the board of directors other than by a meeting of

shareholders, because the schedule is onerous, frequently duplicative, and inconsequential for smaller reporting companies. [40 points; avg. ranking 1.18]

42   Consider recommending for enactment by Congress, the repeal of Exchange Act Section 16(b), but leaving Section 16(a) reporting as is, in order to continue monitoring insider trading. The short-swing profit recovery provisions of Section 16(b) may have a disproportionate impact on the management of smaller public companies who may rely more heavily on equity-based compensation. [39 points; avg. ranking 1.15]

43   The SEC should recommend that the PCAOB conduct a study of the percentage of audit work papers where external auditors rely upon management's Sarbanes-Oxley Act Section 404(a) assessment work papers. [33 points; avg. ranking 0.97]

FORUM RECOMMENDATIONS BY BREAKOUT GROUP

Set forth below are the recommendations of participants in each of the three Forum breakout groups in order of priority, as discussed in footnote 3 on page 10.

Securities-Based Crowdfunding Breakout Group Recommendations

Priority Rank	Recommendation
1	Eliminate the requirement for audited financial statements in crowdfunding offerings, and instead require that financial statements for offerings of $500,000 or more be reviewed by a certified public accountant. [100 points; avg. ranking 2.94]
2	The Commission should provide clarification and a framework on what is considered investment advice for a crowdfunding portal. Portals should be able to provide a labeling mechanism, such as an issue is "hot" or "trending," along with an advanced search feature. [98 points; avg. ranking 2.88]
3	The Commission should provide guidelines to crowdfunding intermediaries as to what constitutes curating deals. [95 points; avg. ranking 2.79]
4	Eliminate the imposition of liability against a crowdfunding platform for the misstatements and omissions of the companies that post on the platform's website, which is proposed in the SEC proposing release for Title III of the JOBS Act at Section II.E.5 of Release No. 33-9470 (Oct. 23, 2013). [94 points; avg. ranking 2.76]
5	Allow crowdfunding portals to create a membership tiered system that will disclose only specific company details (e.g., financial statements) to registered members on the platform. [85 points; avg. ranking 2.50]
6	Clarify whether the intent of proposed Rule 203 of Regulation Crowdfunding is to require all material information to be filed on proposed Form C, or whether "free writing" is permitted to be posted on platforms. [81 points; avg. ranking 2.38]
7A	Allow crowdfunding intermediaries to syndicate deals between platforms by having one lead intermediary host and provide a communication channel to the other funding portals and allow funding portals to share commissions and fees. Transactions must be conducted on the intermediary platform on which they originated. [74 points; avg. ranking 2.18]
7B	Broker-dealers and registered crowdfunding portals should be allowed to share transaction-based compensation in conjunction with Section 4(a)(6) offerings. [74 points; avg. ranking 2.18]
9	Standardize baseline educational materials across crowdfunding portals in order to

establish an industry standard similar to the RESPA administered by the CFPB for the mortgage industry. [70 points; avg. ranking 2.06]

| 10 | Crowdfunding platforms of foreign entities should be allowed to conduct business as a U.S. crowdfunding portal only if the foreign entity forms a partnership with a U.S. crowdfunding portal. [68 points; avg. ranking 2.00] |

| 11 | Allow crowdfunding intermediaries the ability to monitor misstatements on crowdfunding platforms, monitor Q&A commentary and de-rank accordingly as a filtering mechanism. Allow crowdfunding intermediaries the ability to curate based on less objective factors, such as management team experience, over-inflated financials, or size of funding requested, if the funding request is too little to realistically achieve business goals.
[67 points; avg. ranking 1.97] |

| 12 | Another medium other than the Internet should be made acceptable to perform crowdfunding transactions, particularly for local, community-based capital raising efforts. [65 points; avg. ranking 1.91] |

| 13 | Provide a dashboard (tool) that will show updates on intrastate crowdfunding exemptions and federal laws for crowdfunding. [54 points; avg. ranking 1.59] |

| 14A | Standardize deal structures across crowdfunding platforms.
[51 points; avg. ranking 1.50] |

| 14B | Develop educational programs aimed at minority owned firms and investors, and track the effectiveness of those efforts. [51 points; avg. ranking 1.50] |

| 16 | Anyone that invests in a qualifying business, such as a minority, women or veteran owned business, should become eligible for income tax relief based on their investment. [49 points; avg. ranking 1.44] |

Exempt Securities Offerings Breakout Group Recommendations

| 1 | We recommend that the Commission withdraw its proposed amendments to Regulation D, Form D and Rule 156. If the Commission determines not to do so, then we urge that revised proposals be published for further comment to include the following: |

☐ Removal of the harsh penalties for non-compliance;
☐ No requirement for an advance Form D, instead require filing no

    earlier than the date of first sale and a closing or annual filing (if sales were made);

☐   Allow parts of Form D, such as the financing amount, to be confidential;

☐   Require legends and disclosures only when sale terms are communicated;

☐   Rather than requiring the filing of advertising materials, form working groups from advisory bodies to monitor and report to the Commission; and

☐   Clarify the meaning of "general solicitation," and confirm that longstanding economic development events, such as "demo days," do not constitute general solicitation. [112 points; avg. ranking 3.29]

2   Because Rule 506(c) exempt offerings exclude non-accredited friends and family investors, who have traditionally been important participants in small business capital formation, we recommend that the Commission:

☐   Maintain the ability of Rule 506(c) issuers to concurrently offer Section 4(a)(6) crowdfunding securities, as set forth in the proposed rules issued pursuant to the JOBS Act; and

☐   Clarify that an issuer changing from a Rule 506(b) offering to a Rule 506(c) offering may sell to friends and family and other non-accredited investors in a parallel Section 4(a)(6) crowdfunding offering. [105 points; avg. ranking 3.09]

3   We recommend that the Commission not increase the dollar amount thresholds in the accredited investor definition following its review of the definition, as mandated by the Dodd-Frank Act. The Commission has effectively already increased the financial threshold in the definition by removing the value of the primary residence, which resulted in a significant drop in the investor pool from 9% to 7% of U.S. households, thus limiting both capital formation and job creation. At the same time, we recommend that the Commission consider additional separate categories of qualification for accredited investors based on various types of sophistication, for example, by virtue of education, experience or training. [101 points; avg. ranking 2.97]

4A   Based on recent changes resulting from the JOBS Act, private companies will have much more flexibility to remain private longer. As a result, the need for a specific federal exemption for private secondary transactions for shareholders that cannot satisfy Rule 144 has become critical. We recommend that the Commission propose a new federal exemption governing the private resale of restricted securities under Section 4(a)(1) of the Securities Act, commonly referred to as "Section 4(1-1/2)" (or after the JOBS Act amendments to the Securities Act, Section 4(a)(1-1/2)).

[95 points; avg. ranking 2.79]

4B   The Commission should promptly adopt rules implementing Title IV of the JOBS Act that preempt state law review and regulation (but not enforcement) for the issuance of securities thereunder. The Commission should consider, among other means of accomplishing this:

- Making a security offered in reliance upon the Regulation A+ exemption a "covered security" under Section 18(b) of the Securities Act;
- Adopting a "qualified purchaser" definition under Section 18(b)(3) of the Securities Act to include purchasers of securities sold in reliance upon the Regulation A+ exemption;
- Preempting only state regulation that fails to comply with uniform state regulation guidelines adopted by NASAA in consultation with the Commission; or
- Seeking any legislation necessary to so preempt state regulation.

New regulations promulgated under Title IV of the JOBS Act should provide for scaled disclosure based on, among other factors, size of offering, including unaudited financial statements for smaller offerings, and encourage user-friendly techniques, such as Q&A. [95 points; avg. ranking 2.79]

6   The Commission should join with NASAA and FINRA in the effort to implement the basic principles of the American Bar Association Task Force on Private Placement Brokers. Further, to achieve this goal, the Commission should join NASAA and FINRA in developing a timeframe for quarterly or other regular meetings—with specified benchmarks—until a mutually agreeable regime of finder registration and regulation is achieved. [71 points; avg. ranking 2.09]

7   In 1988, pursuant to its exemptive authority, the Commission first issued Rule 701 to allow private companies to sell securities to employees for compensatory purposes. In 1999, the Commission added certain disclosure requirements for sales exceeding $5 million in a 12-month period. Given the Section 12(g) exemptions for employees provided in the JOBS Act, an update of these thresholds is appropriate. We recommend that the Commission raise the dollar threshold for triggering the required disclosures pursuant to a Rule 701 offering from $5 million to no less than $10 million. [69 points; avg. ranking 2.03]

Securities Regulation of Smaller Public Companies Breakout Group Recommendations

Priority Rank	*Recommendation*

1   Repeal the requirement for smaller reporting companies and EGCs to submit financial information in XBRL format for periodic reports and other public filings. [92 points; avg. ranking 2.71]

2   In the voting and prioritization phase of this Forum, the recommendations of each breakout group should be presented separately from those of the other two breakout groups. [83 points; avg. ranking 2.44]

3   Revise the definition of "smaller reporting company" under the Securities Act and Exchange Act to include companies with:

- A public float of up to $250 million; or
- Annual revenues of up to $100 million, so long as their public float is not more than $700 million.

These companies are still generally considered "micro-caps."
[81 points; avg. ranking 2.38]

4   Forum participants report that many broker-dealers will not accept, deposit, clear, sell and/or trade low-priced stocks. They note that FINRA and DTC are requiring broker-dealers to take inordinate responsibility and liability for possible counterfeit certificates, tracking the origin of prior share transfers and monitoring the placement of restricted legends. This issue seriously impacts the participation of investors in financing micro-cap issuers. Through all of its appropriate divisions, the SEC should promptly commence discussions with FINRA and DTC to determine the reasons for, and extent of, these perceived practices, and how such practices can be modified so as not to hamper small business capital formation. [72 points; avg. ranking 2.12]

5   Amend the eligibility requirements in the General Instructions of Form S-3 to permit smaller reporting companies, companies whose common equity securities are not listed on a national securities exchange and companies whose shares are defined as "penny stock" to utilize a registration statement on Form S-3 for primary and secondary offerings, but not for automatically effective shelf offerings, if the companies are current in their Exchange Act reports and have timely filed those reports within the past 12 months. The justifications against expanding Form S-3 usage to smaller public companies have been substantially eliminated with advanced information technology, including EDGAR. This recommendation follows closely the SEC's own proposed rule in 2007 to revise the eligibility requirements for primary securities offerings on Form S-3. See *Revisions to the Eligibility Requirements for Primary Securities Offerings on Forms S-3 and F-3*, Release No. 33-8812 (June 20, 2007). [70 points; avg. ranking 2.06]

6A   Support the ongoing efforts of Nasdaq OMX Group Inc. and NYSE Euronext to widen "tick sizes" to increments of $0.05 for smaller reporting company stock trading. [69 points; avg. ranking 2.03]

6B   Permit "forward incorporation by reference" in registration statements on Form S-1 by all companies. Current practices to supplement an effective registration statement add little or nothing to the availability or quality of subsequent public information provided by issuers. [69 points; avg. ranking 2.03]

8   Consider recommending for enactment by Congress an amendment to the definition of an "emerging growth company" in Section 2(a)(19) of the Securities Act to provide the same benefits that are applicable to EGCs pursuant to the JOBS Act to companies that would have qualified as an EGC, but for the fact that their initial public offerings were declared effective on or prior to December 8, 2011. Congress may accomplish this by amending the definition of an EGC in paragraph (B) of Section 2(a)(19) to add language that states companies whose IPOs were declared effective on or prior to December 8, 2011, may be treated as EGCs starting as of the date of this amendment so as to give effectively to these companies a full 5 years of potential EGC eligibility. [66 points; avg. ranking 1.94]

9   Amend the cover pages of Form 10-K and Form 10-Q to permit registrants to provide the various alternative URL addresses and locations where corporate information may be disseminated by the registrant (e.g., Facebook, Twitter, Tumblr, Instagram and LinkedIn) and, provide that any such postings shall constitute public dissemination for purposes of Regulation FD.
[65 points; avg. ranking 1.91]

10   Extend the disclosure exemptions and scaled or phased-in disclosure obligations that are provided to EGCs under the JOBS Act to all smaller reporting companies, unless there is a significant policy reason for not doing so, including the following requirements:

- The requirement in Exchange Act Section 14A(a) to conduct shareholder advisory votes on executive compensation and on the frequency of such votes;
- The requirement in Exchange Act Section 14A(b) to provide disclosure about and conduct shareholder advisory votes on golden parachute compensation;
- The requirement in Section 953(b) of the Dodd-Frank Act, as promulgated by the Commission in Item 402 of Regulation S-K, to provide disclosure of the ratio of the median annual total compensation of all employees of the registrant to the annual total compensation of the chief executive officer;
- The requirement in Exchange Act Section 14(i) to provide disclosure

of the relationship between executive compensation and issuer financial performance;

☐   In the case of a new or revised financial accounting standard that has different compliance dates for public and private companies, the deferral of compliance with any such financial accounting standard until the date that a private company is required to comply; and

☐   Any rules of the PCAOB requiring mandatory audit firm rotation or a supplement to the auditor's report in which the auditor would be required to provide additional information about the audit and the financial statements of the registrant. [64 points; avg. ranking 1.88]

11   Prohibit the PCAOB from requiring any report or procedure similar to a supplement to the auditor's report in which the auditor would be required to provide additional information about the audit and the financial statements of the issuer, such as a report on "critical audit matters" for the auditors of smaller reporting companies and emerging growth companies. [62 points; avg. ranking 1.82]

12   Given the dwindling number of market-makers willing to submit FINRA Form 211 for trading the shares of smaller publicly reporting companies on the over-the-counter market, the SEC's Division of Trading and Markets should encourage FINRA to allow payment by an issuer of a fixed fee to a market-maker to compensate the market-maker for its time and effort involved in required due diligence, form preparation and related expenses. [59 points; avg. ranking 1.74]

13   As has been generally recommended since 2008, Rule 144(i) should be amended to provide a shell company relief two years after filing a Form 8-K to report that it is no longer a shell company. [56 points; avg. ranking 1.65]

14A   Through all applicable divisions of the SEC, take steps with the national securities exchanges to lower to $15 million the current $40 million minimum required size of a public offering following a reverse merger of an issuer to eliminate the so-called "seasoning" requirement that delays listing the securities of that issuer for more than one year, notwithstanding otherwise meeting all other quantitative and qualitative listing requirements. [55 points; avg. ranking 1.62]

14B   Eliminate the applicability to smaller reporting companies of rules mandating disclosure with respect to conflict minerals, as well as reports by natural resource extraction issuers, concerning payments made to a foreign government or the U.S. federal government in order to further the commercial development of oil, natural gas or minerals, as such rules would be cost prohibitive for smaller natural resource companies. [55 points; avg. ranking 1.62]

14C   Add a general instruction to Regulation S-K that permits smaller reporting companies to omit disclosure required pursuant to a line item in Regulation S-K in the event that such disclosure is not material from the perspective of a reasonable investor. This general instruction should contain language similar to that in Rule 502(b)(2) of Regulation D, which limits the disclosure required to be provided to the purchaser by an issuer "to the extent material to an understanding of the issuer, its business, and the securities being offered." This would add an element of principles-based disclosure to Regulation S-K. [55 points; avg. ranking 1.62]

17   Provide a final rule as to when public companies are required to adopt the new 2013 Framework of the COSO, and provide a one-year delay for required implementation of the rule by smaller reporting companies. [53 points; avg. ranking 1.56]

18   The SEC should repeal the requirement to file an information statement pursuant to Section 14(f) of the Exchange Act and Rule 14f-1 thereunder, concerning notice of change in the majority of the board of directors other than by a meeting of shareholders, because the schedule is onerous, frequently duplicative, and inconsequential for smaller reporting companies. [40 points; avg. ranking 1.18]

19   Consider recommending for enactment by Congress, the repeal of Exchange Act Section 16(b), but leaving Section 16(a) reporting as is, in order to continue monitoring insider trading. The short-swing profit recovery provisions of Section 16(b) may have a disproportionate impact on the management of smaller public companies who may rely more heavily on equity-based compensation. [39 points; avg. ranking 1.15]

20   The SEC should recommend that the PCAOB conduct a study of the percentage of audit work papers where external auditors rely upon management's Sarbanes-Oxley Act Section 404(a) assessment work papers. [33 points; avg. ranking 0.97]

BREAKOUT GROUP PARTICIPANTS

The participants identified below took part either in person or by telephone conference call in the Forum afternoon breakout groups on November 21, 2013. These participants formulated the Forum recommendations set forth beginning on page 10 and were later given an opportunity to participate in a poll to prioritize the recommendations.

Securities-Based Crowdfunding Offerings Breakout Group

Gabriela Aguero
Financial Industry Regulatory Authority
Rockville, Maryland

Joseph Becker
Financial Industry Regulatory Authority
Rockville, Maryland

Amiel Bent
Test Tutor Publishing, LLC
Reston, Virginia

Elizabeth Bleakley
Kopecky, Schumacher & Bleakley, P.C.
Chicago, Illinois

David Bloom
Saint George Consulting, Inc.
Vienna, Virginia

Arturo Bohorquez

Philip Brown
Gopher-Homes
Washington, D.C.

Daryl Bryant
StartupValley
Saddle Brook, New Jersey

Jason Burmer
EarlyShares.com, Inc.
Miami, Florida

Raymond Burrascsa
Colorado Crowdfunding Meetup
Denver, Colorado

David Burton
The Heritage Foundation
Washington, D.C.

Sarah Chopnick
SecondMarket, Inc.
New York, New York

Tad Cook
Cook Business Law, PLLC
Charlotte, North Carolina

Alixe Cormick
Venture Law Corporation
Vancouver, British Columbia
Canada

Andrew Dix
Crowded Media Group, LLC
Cleveland, Ohio

Richard Ellenbogen
Richardson & Patel, LLP
New York, New York

Douglas Ellenoff
Ellenoff, Grossman & Schole, LLP
New York, New York

Steve Ferrando
CrowdClear
New York, New York

Jay Finch
U.S. Treasury Department
Washington, D.C.

Jillien Williams Flores
Porterfield, Lowenthal, Fettig & Sears, LLC
Washington, D.C.

Millissa Foster

Jonathan D. Gworek
Morse, Barnes-Brown & Pendleton, PC
Waltham, Massachusetts

Eileen Chu Hing
Zios Corporation
Philadelphia, Pennsylvania

Douglas E. Haas
Benesch Friedlander
Cleveland, Ohio

Alyn Hadar
U.S. Pan Asian American Chamber of
  Commerce
Washington, D.C.

Sara Hanks
CrowdCheck, Inc.
Alexandria, Virginia

Vincent Harris

Stuart Hoeke
Chuckey, Tennessee

Charles Hopkins
RMD Holdings, LLC
Washington, D.C.

Louise Howells
University of the District of Columbia
David A. Clarke School of Law
Washington, D.C.

Michael Howley
Quantarus Capital Partners, LLC
Charlotte, North Carolina

Kenneth Isaacs
University of the District of Columbia
David A. Clarke School of Law
Washington, D.C.

Rick Johnson
Lake Research Partners
Washington, D.C.

Mary Juetten
Traklight.com
Phoenix, Arizona

Ramkrishna Kasargod
SCORE Memphis Chapter 068
Memphis, Tennessee

Pesach Klein
Community Development Law Clinic
University of the District of Columbia
David A. Clarke School of Law
Washington, D.C.

Rebecca Knutson
Financial Industry Regulatory Authority
Rockville, Maryland

Jeffrey Koeppel
Elias, Matz, Tiernan & Herrick, LLP
Washington, D.C.

Tony Lawrence
National Rural Utilities Cooperative Finance
  Corporation
Dulles, Virginia

Phillip Laycock
Grassi & Co.
New York, New York

Carmen Lobis
Crowdfunding for Growth
West Chester, Pennsylvania

Heather Schwarz-Lopes
EarlyShares
Miami, Florida

Kimberly A. Lowe
Fredrikson & Byron, PA
Minneapolis, Minnesota

Charles Luzar
Crowded Media Group
Beachwood, Ohio

Lora Manson
Tennessee Securities Division
Nashville, Tennessee

Joseph R. Martinez
Morse, Barnes-Brown & Pendleton, PC
Waltham, Massachusetts

Carolyn Meade
Moore & Van Allen, PLLC
Charlotte, North Carolina

Theodore Miles
D.C. Department of Insurance,
  Securities & Banking
Washington, D.C.

Christopher Morley
Financial Industry Regulatory Authority
Washington, D.C.

Robin Prager
Board of Governors of the
  Federal Reserve System
Washington, D.C.

Georgia Quinn
Seyfarth Shaw, LLP
New York, New York

Rene Redwood
Redwood Enterprise, LLC
Washington, D.C.

Tony Reynolds
A Kickin Crowd
Columbus, Ohio

Frederick Rice
The Nauset Group, Inc.
Brewster, Massachusetts

Timothy Tardibono
Innovation Policy Solutions, LLC
Oklahoma City, Oklahoma

Melissa Tucker
D.A.R. Partners, LLC
McLean, Virginia

Bradford Voegeli
Community Development Law Clinic
University of the District of Columbia
David A. Clarke School of Law
Washington, D.C.

Kim Wales
Wales Capital
New York, New York

D. Clinton Webb
OXiGENE, Inc.
South San Francisco, California

Fidencio Yzaguirre

Exempt Securities Offerings Breakout Group

Peter Allen
New York, New York

Edward Alterman
Fried, Frank, Harris, Shriver &
  Jacobson, LLP
New York, New York

Richard Alvarez
Law Office of Richard I. Alvarez
Melville, New York

Steven Anthony Behar
Behar Law Group, PLLC
Bayside, New York

David Burton
The Heritage Foundation
Washington, D.C.

Sarah Chopnick
SecondMarket, Inc.
New York, New York

Faith Colish
Carter Ledyard & Milburn, LLP
New York, New York

Alixe Cormick
Venture Law Corporation
Vancouver, British Columbia
Canada

Molly Diggins
Monument Group, Inc.
Boston, Massachusetts

Douglas Dziak
Nixon Peabody
Washington, D.C.

Nancy Fallon-Houle
Levenfeld Pearlstein, LLC
Chicago, Illinois

Rick Fleming
North American Securities
  Administrators Association, Inc.
Washington, D.C.

Jillien Williams Flores
Porterfield, Lowenthal & Fettig, LLC
Washington, D.C.

Hank Gracin
Gracin & Marlow, LLP
New York, New York
Boca Raton, Florida

Peter Haller
Committee on Financial Services
U.S. House of Representatives
Washington, D.C.

Martin A. Hewitt, Attorney at Law
East Brunswick, New Jersey

Charles Hopkins
RMD Holdings, LLC
Washington, D.C.

Michael Howley
Quantarus Capital Partners, LLC
Charlotte, North Carolina

Barbara Jones
Greenberg Taurig, LLP
Boston, Massachusetts

Erik Kantz
Arnstein & Lehr, LLP
Chicago, Illinois

Michele Kulerman
Skadden, Arps, Slate, Meagher &
  Flom, LLP
Washington, D.C.

Ford Ladd
Law Offices of Ford C. Ladd
Alexandria, Virginia

Gerald Laporte
Arlington, Virginia

Bridget Lau

Wayne Lee
Lee Lowinger, PC
McLean, Virginia

Wayne Leung

Traci Mach
Board of Governors of the
  Federal Reserve System
Washington, D.C.

Jessica Marlin
Ropes & Gray, LLP
New York, New York

Christopher Mirabile
Launchpad Venture Group, LLC
Boston, Massachusetts

D.J. Paul
Gate Global Impact
Cold Spring Harbor, New York

Janet Rosenblum
Crowdnetic
New York, New York

Michael Sauvante
The Commonwealth Group
Youngstown, Ohio

Andy Shawber
Summit Law Group, PLLC
Seattle, Washington

Eric Stein
Szaferman, Lakind, Blumstein & Blader, PC
Lawrenceville, New Jersey

Jodi Stevens
Somerset Capital
Denver, Colorado

Timothy Tardibono
Innovation Policy Solutions, LLC
Oklahoma City, Oklahoma

Joe Theis
Goodwin Proctor, LLP
Boston, Massachusetts

Annemarie Tierney
SecondMarket, Inc.
New York, New York

Joseph Toner
Reed Smith, LLP
Washington, D.C.

Todd A. Torquato
River's Edge Alliance Group, LLC
Pittsburgh, Pennsylvania

Christopher Tyrrell
OfferBoard
Princeton, New Jersey

Chris Walters
Small Business Investor Alliance
Washington, D.C.

Freeman White
Launcht.com
Boston, Massachusetts

Gregory Yadley
Shumaker, Loop & Kendrick, LLP
Tampa, Florida

Jack Yu

Paul Zeller
FisherBroyles
New York, New York

**Securities Regulation of Smaller
Public Companies Breakout Group**

Gabriela Aguero
Financial Industry Regulatory Authority
Rockville, Maryland

Jurgita Ashley
Thompson Hine, LLP
Cleveland, Ohio

Joseph Becker
Financial Industry Regulatory Authority
Washington, D.C.

Drew Connolly
IBA Capital Funding
New York, New York

Charles Crain
Biotechnology Industry Organization
Washington, D.C.

David Feldman
Richardson & Patel, LLP
New York, New York

Spencer Feldman
Olshan Frome Wolosky, LLP
New York, New York

David Grossman
GBH CPAs, PC
Houston, Texas

Alyn Hadar
U.S. Pan Asian American Chamber of
  Commerce
Washington, D.C.

Natalie Hairston
ENGlobal
Houston, Texas

Daniel Kim
Stradling Yocca Carlson & Rauth, PC
Santa Monica, California

Moshe Levitin
Leshkowitz & Company, LLP
New York, New York

Sonia Luna
Aviva Spectrum
Los Angeles, California

Eric Marion
Silver, Freedman, Taff & Tiernan, LLP
Washington, D.C.

William C. McDowell
East Carolina University
Greenville, North Carolina

Christopher Morley
Financial Industry Regulatory Authority
Washington, D.C.

Brian Murphy
Washington, D.C.

Mezaun Norman
TeleFix Communications Holdings, Inc.
Dallas, Texas

Mark Orenstein
Eaton & Van Winkle, LLP
New York, New York

Jaydip Panchal
Panatec Corporation
Manalapan, New Jersey

Chris Russell
Subcommittee on Capital Markets and
  Government Sponsored Enterprises
Committee on Financial Services
U.S. House of Representatives
Washington, D.C.

Eric Stein
Szaferman, Lakind, Blumstein & Blader, PC
Lawrenceville, New Jersey

Jodi Stevens
Somerset Capital
Denver, Colorado

Arielle Schwartz
Community Development Legal Clinic
University of the District of Columbia
David A. Clarke School of Law
Washington, D.C.

Eustace Uku
Exico, Inc.
Pittsburgh, Pennsylvania

Michael Vasilios
OTC Markets Group, Inc.
Washington D.C.

Ann Yvonne Walker
Wilson Sonsini Goodrich & Rosati, LLP
Palo Alto, California

Paul Zeller
FisherBroyles
New York, New York

www.ingramcontent.com/pod-product-compliance
Lightning Source LLC
Chambersburg PA
CBHW080624180526
45168CB00007B/3041